Richard Mocket

God and the King, or,

A dialogue shewing that our Soveraign Lord the King of England

Richard Mocket

God and the King, or,
A dialogue shewing that our Soveraign Lord the King of England

ISBN/EAN: 9783337869373

Printed in Europe, USA, Canada, Australia, Japan

Cover: Foto ©ninafisch / pixelio.de

More available books at **www.hansebooks.com**

G O D

AND THE

KING:

OR, A

DIALOGUE

SHEWING,

That Our Soveraign Lord the King of
ENGLAND, being immediate under God
within his Dominions, doth rightly claim
whatſoever is required by the Oath
of Allegiance.

Formerly compiled and printed by the eſpecial Command of
King JAMES (of bleſſed memory;) and now commanded to be reprinted and publiſhed by his Majeſties Royal Proclamation, for the Inſtruction of all his Majeſties Subjects in
their Duty and Allegiance.

LONDON,
Imprinted by his Majeſties ſpecial Priviledge and
Command, 1663.

THE
CONTENTS
OF THIS
DIALOGUE.

✹✹✹✹✹✹✹✹✹✹✹✹ : ✹✹✹✹✹✹✹

G O D
AND THE
K I N G:
O R, A
D I A L O G U E,
SHEWING,

That our Soveraign Lord the King
of *England*, being immediate under
God within his Dominions, doth
rightly claim whatsoever is
required by the

OATH of ALLEGIANCE.

Theodidaĉtus.

YOU are well met friend *Philalethes*;
your countenance and gesture im-
port that your thoughts are much
busied : what may be the occasion
of these Meditations ?

Philalethes. *Somewhat I heard
this Evening-Prayer from our Pastor in his Catechistical Expositions
upon the fifth Commandment,* "Honor thy Father, and Exodus 20.
thy

thy Mother : *who taught, that under these pious and re-*
verent appellations of Father *and* Mother *are comprised*
not onely our natural Parents, but likewise all higher Pow-
ers ; and especially such as have Soveraign Authority, as
the Kings and Princes of the Earth.

Theodidactus. Is this Doctrine so strange unto you,
as to make you muse thereat ?

Philalethes. God forbid ; for I am well assured of the
truth thereof, both out of the Word of God, and from the
Light of Reason. The sacred Scriptures do stile Kings
*and Princes the * nursing Fathers of the Church, and*
therefore the nursing Fathers also of the Common-weal :
these two Societies having so mutual a dependance, that
the welfare of the one is the prosperity of the other.

* Isaiah 49.

And the Evidence of Reason teacheth, that there is a
stronger and higher bond of Duty between Children and the
Father of their Countrey, than the Fathers of private Fa-
milies. These procure the good onely of a few, and not
without the assistance and protection of the other, Who are
the common Foster-fathers of thousands of Families, of
whole Nations and Kingdoms, that they may live under
them an honest and peaceable life.

There being so firm and near an Obligement of Subjects
in Duty and Obedience unto their Prince, I could not but
seriously meditate with my self, or rather enter into some
thoughtful admiration, how there should be any so far un-
natural, and forgetful of their many ways bounden and in-
bred Duty, as to enforce his most excellent Majesty to secure
himself of his Subjects Loyalty and Allegiance by a solemn
Oath.

Theodidactus. Such is the general pravity and cor-
ruption of men, that in most Kingdoms, and Common-
weals, there have ever risen some seditious *Corahs,* and
rebellious *Sheba's.*

Philal. It may be upon some extraordinary provocation
by the cruel Oppressions and insolent Tyrannies of Gover-
nors.

                                              Theodi-

Theodid. Nay, frequently, men, onely out of pride and ambition, or out of a blinde and intemperate zeal, or from the effect of both (when they are checked by the raigns of Government) repining discontent, have sown the tares of Sedition against the most vertuous and religious Princes; and ungratefully plotted their ruine, even when they have been most propitious and indulgent towards them.

What Prince was ever more merciful and compassionate then King *David*, as being fashioned and framed wholly according to his heart who is the God of Mercy and Compassion? yet (a) wicked Sheba *the son of* Bichri *(a)* 2 Sam. 20. *lifted up his hand against him, and blew the Trumpet* of Schism and Sedition to rent his Kingdom from him.

That peaceful and moderate Emperor *Augustus*, honored by his Enemies for his Princely vertues, was assailed (b) ten several times by Conspirators. *Vespasian*, even (b) Suet.cap. 19 composed of mildness and clemency, (c) *had daily Trea-* (c) Suet.cap. 25 *sons* against him; and his son *Titus*, for his pleasing and amiable vertues, termed by (d) *Suetonius, the love and* (d) Cap. 1. *delight of mankinde*, wanted not a (e) traiterous Ce- (e) Suet. cap. 6. *cina.*

But leaving ancient and forreign, and to instance in modern and domestick Examples (as most powerful to perswade, being fresh in our memories) his Majesties clemency towards the *Romanists*, and Papal Faction, at his happy Entrance into this Kingdom, was rare and admirable; especially if we consider their disloyalty and sanguinary attempts against Queen *Elizabeth* of blessed memory, onely under pretence of promoting their Superstition, whereunto his Majesty was a constant and professed Opposite, as well as his Royal Sister.

In the beginning of Queen *Elizabeths* reign, the (a) Apology of (a) *most part* of such as were addicted to the *Roman* Ecclesiastical *Superstition*, communicating with us in Divine Service, Hierarch.cap.1. lived free from all punishment or molestation, and enjoyed common favors and benefits with other of her

B   Majesties

Majefties loyal Subjects. Of which their practife the Pope being advertifed by fome fervent and zealous *Romanifts*, and that hereby in time his adherents would by little and little wholly confociate themfelves with our Church, and fo all hope would be loft by a home-party, of reducing this Kingdom unto his Subjection, out of which his Predeceffors had gathered fuch rich Treafures.

Anne Domini 1569. 11 Reg. Eliz.

Sand. lib.7. de vifib.Monarch. *Pius Quintus*, to prevent fo great a Damage unto the See of *Rome*, and for this purpofe to make an open Schifm between his devoted Vaffals, and her Majefties dutiful and faithful Subjects, he fent *Moreton*, an *Englifh* Prieft, to declare by his Papal Authority unto the then Earls of *Northumberland* and *Weftmerland*, upon whom multitudes of Popifh People in the North were dependant, that Queen *Elizabeth was an Heretique*, (and therefore that they ought to have no communion with her in civil affairs, much lefs in religious) *becaufe, by being an Heretique, fhe was faln from all Dominion and Power, and they were not compelled to obey her Laws and Commandments.*

(a) Stow in annal, 12 Eliz. Whereupon they raifed an Army of *(a)* four thoufand Footmen, and fix hundred Horfe, for the maintenance of the Liberty of their Confcience, and the Reformation of Religion, pretending *they were driven to take this enterprife in hand, left otherwife Forreign Princes might take it upon them, to the great peril of this Realm:* which Forces were foon vanquifhed, and onely fome chief Confpirators receiving condign punifhment for their Rebellion: other Papifts that did not partake in this feditious commotion (through the gracious difpofition of her Majefty) enjoyed the fame Liberty they did before.

But *Pius Quintus* was neither mitigated by her Majefties clemency, nor daunted with the ill fuccefs of his factious Complices: for being informed that his Projects *(b) Sand.lib.7. vifib.Monarch.* took not that effect he expected *(b) becaufe all the Catholiques knew not that Queen* Elizabeth *was declared an Heretique,* not long after he did publifh a *Bull,* wherein,

one.

out of the fulness of his Power, he denounced Queen Eliza- **Anno Dom.**
beth an Heretique, and that such as did cleave unto her **1570, 12 Eliz.**
should incur his Curse; that she was deprived of all Domi-
nion and Dignity; that her Nobles and People, or any other
that had sworn Obedience unto her, were freed from this
Oath, and from all Allegiance and Fidelity; commanding
them not to obey her Laws upon pain of his Curse. And
that this *Bull* might be the more generally known unto
Romanists, and to gain undoubted credence thereunto, he
caused it to be printed at *Rome,* to be signed by a publique
Notary, sealed with the Seal of his Court; and at length,
being sent into *England,* it was fastened by one *Felton,*
deeply plunged in the *Roman* Superstition, upon the Gates
of the Bishop of *London's* Palace.

And although these Papal thunders and curses of *Pius*
Quintus were but as *(c) the noise of thorns under the pot,* **(c) Ecclef.7.8.**
and vanished like the vapor of smoke; yet *Gregory* the
thirteenth, immediately succeeding *Pius Quintus,* con- **Anno 1578.**
firmed and ratified his *Bull,* erected a * Colledge at *Rome,* **14 Eliz.**
give a Pension to another Colledge at *Doway,* to be receptacles for Fugitives and discontented Persons in *Eng-*
land, to be instructed in School-points of Sedition (as it
is manifest by the Books and Writings of their then chief **(d) See Bristows**
Masters and Oracles *(d) Bristow* and *Allen*) and from **Motives, Mot.**
15.40. and Al-
thence to be secretly conveyed into this Kingdom, to per- **lens Defence,**
swade men they were bound to obey the *Popes Bulls* and **Eng. Catholic.4.**
Excommunications, to renounce their natural Allegiance
unto her Majesty, and take part with any Domestical or
Forreign Power to depose her from her Regal Throne.

The most eminent and principal men of note amongst
these Fugitives were the Jesuites *Campian* and *Parsons,*
who, at the commandment of *Gregory* the thirteenth,
coming towards this Kingdom, desired of him that the
forenamed Bull of *Pius Quintus,* which himself also had
established, might so be understood, *(e) as to binde the* **(e) Instruments**
Queen and the Heretiques (but not the Catholiques) as **of this inter-**
pretation found
matters then stood, but when there might be had a publique **amongst**
Papists.

1580.
About this
time *Persons*
writ the Rea-
fons of Refufal
of going to
Proteftant
Churches; up-
on which wri-
ting (faith the
Apology of the
Ecclefiaftical
Hierarchy)
when many
chief men re-
fufed to go to
Heretical Ser-
vice, there was
called a Parlia-
ment in the
end of the fame
year, and the
Law of twenty
pound a Month
for Recufants
was ordained,
but no capital
Law made a-
gainft Priefts,
or their re-
ceivers.
Anno Dom.
1581. 24 *Reg.*
Eliz.

execution thereof. With thefe Inftructions they entred *England;* and *Saunders* the fame time *Ireland,* with an Army from the *Pope,* to fuccor the Rebel *Defmond.* And as *Saunders* labored by violence and force of Arms to 'enthral mens perfons; fo thefe, with artificial and plaufible perfwafions, to captivate their Souls : and prevailed with many, together with a refufal of communicating with us in the Religious Worfhip of God, to renounce their civil Duty and Allegiance unto their 'Soveraign.

And thus, by the feditious practifes of Jefuites and Priefts, this Seperation of her Majefties Subjects from Divine Service daily increafing, and accompanied with a perilous diffolution of the bond of their civil Obedience ; yet her Majefty, out of her great moderation and incomparable goodnefs of nature, impeached none of thefe rebellious *Seperatifts,* either in their Lives, Lands, Goods, or Liberties ; but only, by a Decree in Parliament, punifhed them with a pecuniary mulct for the time they refufed to come unto the Church, and publifhed a Proclamation for the *Revocation of all fuch as remained beyond the Seas under the colour of ftudy,* to be the *Authors of Treafonable Attempts.*

Wherewith thefe Seed-men of Sedition were no way fuppreffed, but rather did daily multiply, and at length grew unto that height of impiety, as to animate fundry 1582. 25 *Eliz.* defperate perfons, and fons of *Belial* ; as *Arden,** *Parry,* and others of the fame rank, with hope of Eternal Salvation, to lay violent hands upon her Majefties facred perfon : and became principal Agents to incite the King 1583. 26 *Eliz.* of *Spain* (then entring into Hoftility with this Land) to invade the Realm, affuring him to have here a Party of *Romanifts,* ready to affift fuch Power as he fhould fet on Land, for fubduing of this potent Kingdom.

Which unchriftian and unnatural Enterprizes of Fugitive Jefuites and Priefts, covered with the Mantle of Zeal and Religion, enforced her Majefty, after much patience 1584. 27 *Eliz.* and longanimity, to Enact by publique Authority of Parliament,

liament, *That if any Jesuites or Priests, made in parts be-*
yond the Seas, according to the rites of the Roman Church,
came into this Realm, they should be adjudged Traitors,
and suffer as in case of high treason.

All these notorious feditions and rebellions, hatched
and produced by the papal Faction, and their chief-
tains Jefuits and Priefts, out of a zeal to reduce into
this Land the Idolatry of *Rome* ; and the juftice and
equity of the forementioned laws, made by the late re-
nowned *Queen* , to fupprefs and prevent them , were
well known unto his moft excellent Majefty : and therefore at his happy inauguration unto this Kingdom, out
of his own maturenefs of judgment, and grounded per-
fwafion of the Truth, being refolved to tread the fteps
of his Royal Sifter, and by the light of the *Gofpel* to
extinguifh the *Egyptian* darknefs of Popery; he could
not but in his Princely wifdom more then conjecture,
that the like difloyal attempts might be practifed.
againft his facred Dignity and Perfon by thefe *Roma-*
nifts. Notwithftanding, out of his gracious inclination
unto Pity and Mercy, defiring to conquer Evil with
Goodnefs, in the beginning of his Reign he fet at liber- [1603]
ty all Jefuits and Priefts that were imprifoned ; and unto
fuch as lurked in fecret corners of the Land, he gave
them leave openly to profefs themfelves to be fuch : fo
that both by a certain day would depart the Realm.
And as for other recufant Papifts, refufing to partake
with us in the fincere worfhip of GOD, he frees them
from all pecuniary mulcts impofed upon them by the
Law, honored many of them with Knighthood, gave them
free accefs unto his Court and prefence, beftowed equal
favours upon them with their oppofites in Profeffion.
They were not provoked by any tyrannous Cruelty or
Oppreffion unto any feditious Enterprifes.

Philalethes. *Surely no, but rather had juft caufe to*
be truly dutiful, and loyal to his Majefty; who thus did
change deferved Juftice into Mercy and Clemency.

Theo-

Theodidaĉlus. The Mercy indeed and Favour of Kings

(a) Prov. 16. 15. and Princes, is like a (*a*) cloud of the latter rain, and worketh much, even upon mindes not well difpofed. But fome of thefe *Romanifts* were of fo rancorous fpirit, and brutifh ingratitude, that whileft they peaceably injoyed the fore-cited Favours, they did plot a Treafon barbarous for Cruelty, unmatchable in regard of example, the Horrible Deftruĉlion by Gunpowder, of the *King*, *Queen*, their royal Progeny, and the whole Court of Parliament at once.

Philal. *Did the bloody Aĉlors of this monſtrous attempt alledge no motive or reafon thereof ?*

Theod. None but their fanatical zeal to promote the *Romiſh* Religion ; which enraged affeĉlion out of charity is not to be fuppofed to be in all of that Profeffion, and in wifdom to be feared leaft it be in fome, furviving thefe offendors : And therefore, to difcern the one from the other, the Oath of Allegiance (which hath occafioned this our conference) was principally framed.

Philal. *They that will be fo impious as to lift up their hand againſt Gods anointed, little fear the hainous fin of Perjury, and therefore this Oath will not much avail to difcover fuch treacherous Perfons.*

Theod. An Oath is a moft facred Bond, and with a fecret terror, imprinted by the immediate finger of God in the taking thereof, doth fo ftraitly oblige the inmoft Soul and Confcience, that although many men be obdurate unto other grievous Sins, yet they will be tender and fenfible of the violation of an Oath. *Very often (faith Saint*

(Contra mendac. ad Conf. cap. 21.) *Auguftine) men provoke their wives, whom they fufpeĉl to be Adulterous, to clear themfelves by an Oath ; which they would not do, unlefs they did believe that thofe which fear not Adultery may fear Perjury : for indeed (faith he) fome unchaſte women, which have not feared to deceive their hufbands by wantonnefs, have been afraid to ufe God unto them as a witnefs of their Chaſtity.* In the marital Conjunĉlion of the Husband and Wife, there is a lively re-
femblance

femblance of the Obligation of Subjects in civil Allegiance unto their Prince : for as the coupling of the Wife
unto the husband in dutiful Obedience, so of Subjects
unto their Prince in Loyalty and Fidelity, is a very arct
and near Union: and as the *(a)* Husband is the head of (a) 1 Cer.11.3.
the Wife, so is the *(b)* Prince of his Subjects. As there- (b) 1 Sam.15.17
fore experience in the daies of Saint *Augustine* taught,
that Wives did rather dread wilful Perjury, then undu-
tifulness towards their Husbands; so it is now to be pre-
sumed, that many Subjects will abhor the same crying Sin
more then Disobedience.

Philal. *But is there any example in former ages of the
like Oath for the trying of the Loyalty of the Subjects unto
their Soveraign?*

Theod. About a thousand years since, the same Oath
in substance was used in *Spain*, and ratified by the Canons
of diverse famous Councels of *Toledo* : For whereas *Concil. To'es.n.*
there *was a general report, that there was such perfidiouf-* 4.can.74.
*nefs in the mindes of many people of diverse Nations, that
they made no Confcience of keeping their oaths and fidelity
that they had sworn unto their Kings ; but did diffemble a
profeffion of fidelity in their mouthes* (like unto equivoca-
ting Papists) *When they held an impious perfidiousnefs in
their hearts* : the fourth Council of *Toledo* decreed (as (a) Conc'l.Tolet. .
also other *(a)* Councels afterward held in the same 5.c.10.
City) that *(b) whosoever of us, or of all the people through* (b) Can. 74.
all Spain, *shall go about, by any means of conspiracy
or practise, to violate the oath of his fidelity, which he
hath taken for the preservation of his Country, or of the
Kings life ; or who shall attempt to lay vi.lent hands upon
the King ; or to deprive him of his Kingly power ; or by
tyrannical presumption usurp the Soveraignty of the Kingdom ; let him be accurfed in the fight of God the Father,
and of his Angels ; and let him be made and declared a
ftranger from the Catholick Church, which he hath pro-
faned with his perjury.*

Philal. *Hath this oath any agreement and correfpon-
dence*

dence with the Oath of Allegiance unto the Kings Majesty?

Theodidactus. Almoft in every point and circumftance, as you will eafily perceive, if I fhall but read the Oath of Allegiance unto you out of this book which I have in my hand: for the tenor hereof is thus word for word.

I A. B. Do truly and fincerely acknowledge, profefs, teftifie and declare in my confcience before God and the world; That our Soveraign Lord King James is lawful and rightful King of this Realm, and of all other his Majefties Dominions and Countries; and that the Pope, neither of himfelf, nor by any Authority by the Church or See of Rome, or by any other means with any other, hath any power or Authority to depose the King, or to difpose any of his Majefties Kingdoms, or Dominions; or to authorize any Foreign Prince to invade or annoy him, or his Countries; or to difcharge any of his Subjects of their Allegiance and Obedience to his Majefty; or to give licence or leave to any of them to bear Arms, raife tumults, or to offer any violence, or hurt, to his Majefties royal Person, State, or Government, or to any of his Majefties Subjects within his Majefties Dominions.

Also I do fwear from my heart, that notwithftanding any declaration, or fentence of Excommunication, or Deprivation, made, or granted, or to be made, or granted by the Pope, or his Succeffors, or by any Authority, derived, or pretended to be derived from him, or his See, againft the faid King, his Heirs or Succeffors, or any abfolution of the faid Subjects from their obedience: I will bear Faith and true Allegiance to his Majefty, his Heirs and Succeffors, and him and them will defend, to the uttermoft

of

of my power, against all conspiracies and attempts whatsoever, which shall be made against his or their Persons, their Crown and dignity, by reason or colour of any such sentence, or declaration, or otherwise, and will do my best endeavor to disclose and make known unto his Majesty, his Heirs, and Successors, all Treasons, or Traiterous Conspiracies, which I shall know, or hear of, to be against him or any of them.

And I do further swear, that I do from my heart abhor, detest, and abjure, as impious and heretical, this damnable doctrine, and position, That Princes, which be excommunicated or deprived by the Pope, may be deposed, or murthered by their Subjects, or any other whatsoever.

And I do believe, and in Conscience am resolved, that neither the Pope, nor any person whatsoever, hath power to absolve me of this Oath, or any part thereof, which I acknowledge by good and full Authority to be lawfully ministered unto me, and do renounce all pardons and dispensations to the contrary. And all these things I do plainly and sincerely acknowledge and swear, according to these express words by me spoken, and according to the plain and common sense and understanding of the same words, without any equivocation, or mental evasion, or secret reservation whatsoever. And I do make this recognition and acknowledgement heartily, willingly, and truly, upon the true faith of a Christian: So help me God.

Philal. *There is indeed between this Oath, and the former, established by the Councels of* Toledo, *a perfect harmony, if we respect the substance of the matter in them, save that the former Oath is more general and concise, the latter more diffuse and particular. And therefore I would intreat you, for my more clear and distinct apprehension thereof, to*

resolve

resolve it into the several heads and branches of which it doth consist.

Theod. I shall presently give you satisfaction herein. In an Oath there is the *matter* or *truth* which we swear, or the *form* and *manner* how we are to swear. The *manner* of taking this Oath is *to swear plainly, sincerely,* and without *all equivocation, mental reservation, or secret interpretation,* in (a) *Justice, Judgement, and Truth* ; otherwise then that infamous Heretique (b) *Arius* swore, who being demanded by the Emperor, whether he would subscribe unto the *Nicene Faith,* which condemned his Heresie, denying the Godhead of Christ ; he forthwith yielded hereunto : and being further required by the Emperor (suspecting his dissimulation) to swear unto the same faith, he writ his own Heretical Confession, subscribed it, hid it in his bosom ; and then, having a mental relation unto his Confession, he took an Oath that he had truly and from his heart subscribed. In which perfidious action, the wretched Heretique was either ignorant, or wilfully forgetful, that *by* (c) *whatsoever art of words any man sweareth, yet God, who is the witness of the conscience, accepteth it, as he doth to whom the Oath is made.*

(a) Jer.4.2.
(b) Socrat.
Hist.l.1.c.25.
N: 3.Hist.
lib.8.c.5.

(c) I Edn.
Hispal.Senten.
l.1.c.31.Bern.
de inter. Dom.
c.15.

The matter or main subject of this Oath, which is the principal thing whereof I conceive you desire to have a more distinct and full understanding, may to this purpose be resolved into these ensuing assertions.

1. Our Soveraign Lord King James is the lawful King of this Kingdom, and of all other his Majesties Dominions and Countries.

2. The Pope, neither by his own Authority, nor by any other Authority of the Church, or of the See of Rome, nor by any other means, with any others help, can depose his Majesty.

3. The Pope cannot dispose of any of his Majesties Kingdoms and Dominions.

4. The Pope cannot give Authority to any

for

Foreign Prince to invade his Dominions.

5. The Pope cannot discharge his Subjects of their Allegiance unto his Majesty.

6. The Pope cannot give licence to one or more of his Subjects to bear arms against him.

7. The Pope cannot give leave to any of his Subjects to offer violence unto his Royal Person, or to his Government, or to any of his Majesties Subjects.

8. Although the Pope shall by sentence excommunicate, or depose his Majesty, or absolve his Subjects from their obedience, notwithstanding they are to bear faith and true Allegiance unto his Majesty.

9. If the Pope shall by sentence excommunicate or depose his Majesty; nevertheless his Subjects are bound to defend his Person and Crown against all attempts and conspiracies whatsoever.

10. If the Pope shall give out any sentence of excommunication, or deprivation against his Majesty; notwithstanding his Subjects are bound to reveal all Conspiracies, and Treasons against his Majesty, which shall come to their hearing and knowledge.

11. It is heretical and detestable, to hold, that Princes, being excommunicated by the Pope, may be deposed or murthered by their Subjects, or any other.

12. The Pope hath not power to absolve his Majesties Subjects from their Oath of Allegiance, or any part thereof.

Philal. *By these assertions thus distinctly proposed, I confess I do conceive the principal contents of the Oath more clearly then before: But I would not onely have a full and through apprehension of this Oath, but likewise upon any occasion, for the more expedite performance of my duty unto his excellent Majesty, readily remember it, which I shall be.*

the

the better able to do, if you would be pleased to reduce this multiplicity of assertions unto some fewer heads.

Theod. This may easily be accomplished: There are two special grounds or foundations of true Soveraignty in our gracious Lord the King. The one, *that receiving his Authority onely from God, he hath no Superior to punish or chastise him but God alone.* The other, *that the bond of his Subjects, in obedience unto his Sacred Majesty is inviolable, and cannot be dissolved.* These two general heads (presupposing the undoubted truth of the first assertion [*Our Soveraign Lord King* James *is the Lawful King of this Kingdom, and all other his Dominions and Countries*]·because the most * seditious impugners of of his Majesties Crown and dignity freely acknowledge it) comprise all the other assertions, as even now I severally proposed them out of the Oath of Allegiance.

For to begin then with the first head: seeing that when God would denounce his most heavy Judgments against wicked Kings that transgrest his Law, as against *Saul* and *Rehoboam,* he threatneth them with renting their Kingdoms from them, and making their houses desolate ; the *deposing of a King,* the *disposing of his Dominions* unto another, *the hostile invading of his Countries,* must needs be a grievous Chastisement: And therefore if his Majesty hath no Superior beside God to punish him, the Pope as his *Superior* cannot *by any means* whatsoever *depose him, dispose of his Dominions, invade his Countries,* which is the effect and substance of the second, third, and fourth Assertions.

Philal. *Doth the same general ground of his Majesties Kingly Soveraignty comprehend the rest of the assertions ?*

Theod. No, for they are all contained within the limits of the second principle of Regal Soveraignty, *That the Bond of the Kings Subjects in Obedience unto his Majesty is inviolable, and cannot be dissolved.* This will be evident unto you by a compendious recital of the chief parts and duties of Allegiance from a Subject to his

Prince.

Prince. And we cannot learn thefe duties from a better
Mafter than God himfelf, who hath fo exactly taught
them in his facred Word.

The general duty which God enjoyneth upon all men,
to efchew evill and do good, is diffufed through the particular duties of every man ; whether it be the duty of a
fervant unto his Mafter, of a fon unto his Father, or of
a fubject unto his Prince. And in the Allegiance of a
Subject unto his Soveraign, the *Evill* he is to *efchew* is
evill in Action, for he is not to (b) *touch* him with any (b) Pfal. 105.
hurtful touch, nor to (c) *ftretch out his hand againft his* (c) 1 Sam. 15.
facred Perfon, nor fo much as to affright, or difgrace him,
by cutting the lap of his Garment : *Evil in Words*, for
(d, *he is not to curfe his Ruler* : *Evill* in Cogitations, for (d) Exod. 11.
he is not to (e) *curfe the King in his thought*. So likewife (e) Eccl. 10.
the good which he is to do, out of Obedience unto his
Prince, is in *Deed*, by (f) *paying Tribute* unto him for (f) Rom. 13.
his Regal fupport, by fighting his Battels with *Joab*, ad-
venturing his life with *David*, to vanquifh his Enemies :
in Speech, by revealing with religious (g) *Mordecai* the (g) Efter 2.
treafonable defignments of *Bigan* and *Terefh*, by pour-
ing out prayers (h) and fupplications for his welfare : in (h) 1 Tim. 2.
Thought, by efteeming and honoring him from the heart,
and out of (i) Confcience, as the (k) *anointed of the Lord*, (i) Rom. 13.
Gods holy Ordinance, and Minifter, and as a (l God upon (k) Efay 45.
earth : for this is to obey him for the (m) *Lords fake*, (l) Pfal. 82.
to fear God, and *honour the King* (n) ; when we fear God, (m) 1 Pet. 2.
by whom the (o) King reigneth, and his throne is efta- (n) 1 Pet. 2.
blifhed. (o) Prov. 8.

Now if the Subjects of our Soveraign, out of their *Al-*
legiance unto his Majefty, are not to lay violent hands
upon his facred Perfon, but to fuccor and defend him
even with the hazzard of their lives : not to curfe him
with their tongues ; but to blefs him by prayers and fupplications, and preferve him by difcovering all attempts
againft his life and dignity : not to harbour in their
Souls any evil thought of him ; but from their heart to
honour him as Gods Vicegerent here upon earth : and

the *Bond of this Allegiance* (as the second ground of *Kingly Soveraignty averreth*) *is inviolable, and cannot by any means be diffolved:* then, although the Pope doth arrogantly prefume to *difcharge them from their Allegiance unto his Majefty, to abfolve them from their Oaths of Obedience, to give licence unto them to bear Arms againft him, and offer violence unto his perfon, to excommunicate and depofe his Majefty;* all thefe impious and irreligious practifes are in vain; and notwithftanding, they are *not to depofe, or murther his Majefty, or any way to offer violence unto his facred Perfon, Crown, and Dignity; but to defend him againft all Confpiracies, to reveal all Treafons againft his Majefty, and bear unto him faith and true Allegiance.*

Philalethes. *I do now fully conceive how the two props and pillars of fupreme Authority in his excellent Majefty, which you have propofed, do briefly and as it were by way of Epitome, comprife all the chief and material points of the Oath: and although I am moft affured in my Confcience of their firmnefs and immoveable Stability in the truth; yet to be the more enabled for the juftifying of them unto others, I would requeft you to fhew how thefe pillars are fupported, and upon what foundations they are built.*

Theod. Hereunto I do willingly condefcend, and will firft difcover unto you the foundations of the firft Prop, or Pillar; *Our Soveraign Lord King JAMES, receiving his Authority onely from God, hath no Superior to chaftife and punifh him but God alone.*

The ancient practice of this Kingdom is clear for this Truth: *Bracton,* * twenty years chief Juftice under *Henry* the third, in his * Cuftoms of *England* faith; *There are under the King freemen, and fervants are fubject unto his power, as alfo whatfoever is under him; and he himfelf is fubject to no man, but onely unto God.* And again, *if there be any offence committed by him; forafmuch as there is no breve to enforce or conftrain him, there may be fupplication made that he would correct and amend his fault: which if he fhall not do, it is abundantly fufficient punifhment*

for

* *fol.* 1.
* 1 Concerz.
   rubric 1. 55.

Et ipfe fub nullo, fed tantum fub D.o.

for him that he is to expect God a revenger : for no man
may presume, *judicially to examine his doings, much less *Disquirere.
to oppose them by Force and Violence.* And this is no othe.
Kingly Soveraignty then God himself hath given unto his
Majesty: *I counsel thee* (saith God by the mouth of (p)*So-* (p) Eccl. 8.
lomon) *to keep the Kings Commandment, and that in re-
gard of the Oath of God: be not hasty to go out of his sight,
stand not in an evil thing, for he doth Whatsoever pleaseth
him.* *Where the Word of a King is, there is power; and who
may say unto him, What dost thou?* An evident testimony,
that as Kings are subject unto God, whom (q) *We are* (q) Acts 5.
to obey rather then men ; so they are subject onely unto
God, and have no mortal man their Superior, who may
require of them an account of their doings, and punish
them by any judicial Sentence.

And this divine Verity was not onely taught by *Solomon*, but likewise by his father *David*; who, out of a
Consideration of the eminency of this Regal Authority,
subject onely unto the severe Judgment of God, poureth (r) Psal. 51. 6.
out before him this penitent Confession: (r) *Against the,* *Apolog. Da-*
against thee onely have I sinned. *Against thee onely : for* *Epist. 7. Epist. &*
he was a King (saith * Ambrose) *not bound unto Law,* *See 16. in Psal.*
because Kings are free from the bond of Crimes, and are not *18. with whom*
called unto punishment by any Law, being safe by the power *da. Glossa. ord.*
of Command : therefore David sinned not against man, un- *Euthym: in 51.*
to whom he was not obnoxious, in regard of Punishment; *Ps. & Dydimus,*
but of Admonition onely, and Reproof, uttered in the *Aurea catena.*
Name, and by the Authority of God himself. *in 50. Psalmos.*

Hereupon the Prophet *Nathan*, having used this Pre- *Leo 4. 2. n.r.c.*
face (*Thus saith the Lord*) *admonished King* David *that* *Non si compe-*
he should expiate his sin by Repentance , *but he gave no* *tenter.2 Sam.12:*
*sentence against him whereby according to the Law he
might be adjudged unto Death.* For if *Nathan* had given
any such sentence against *David*, he should have had
power to deprive him of his Life, and so of that which
he enjoyed by his Life, his Regal Authority; which God
only can take away from Princes, because he alone bestow-
eth it upon them.

Fos.

For from whence have they received their Soveraignty to be here upon earth as gods over men ? God himself

(s) Pſal. 8ʒ. anſwereth, (ſ) *I (and not any creature whatſoever) have ſaid, ye are are Gods :* and as by my Word the world was made ; ſo are ye appointed by the ſame Word to rule the world. Who hath given unto them their Kingdoms ?

(s, Dan. 4. the moſt High, (t) *he ruleth in the kingdom of men, and giveth it to whomſoever he will.* What power hath ſeated them in their Thrones ? The power of the Almighty,

(u) Job 36. (u) *Reges* (as the vulgar Tranſlation readeth it) *collocat in ſolio,* he placeth Kings in the Throne. And by whom do they ſway their Scepters, and govern their Kingdoms ?

(x) Prov. 8. By Gods ſpecial Authority, (x) *by me (ſaith God himſelf) do Kings reign, and decree juſtice,* by his immediate power

(y) Pſal. 47. who is (y) *Lord and King of all the earth.* And to deſcend unto particulars, Doth not God by the mouth of his

(z) 2 Sam. 12. Prophet *Nathan* tell *David,* (z) *I anointed thee King over*

(a) 1 King. 2. *Iſrael?* doth not *Solomon* acknowledge, that (a) *the Lord hath eſtabliſhed him, and ſet him on the throne of his father David ?* was it not the ſaying of the Prophet *Ahija* in the

(b) 1 King. 11. perſon of God unto *Jeroboam,* (b) *I will give the kingdom unto thee?* Neither the kingdom only, and the power of Princes, but all things elſe proper unto them, are after a

(c) Pſal. 21. peculiar manner Gods. Their (c) *Crown,* their (d) *A-*
(d) Pſal. 89. *nointing,* their (e) *Scepter* and *Throne* are Gods ; and
(e) 2 Chron. 9. their perſons, adorned with all theſe, are ſo Divine and

(f) 2 Sam. 14. Sacred, that they themſelves are the (f) *Angels of God,*
(g) Pſal. 82. and (g) *ſons of the moſt High.*

Philal. *If the Perſons of Princes are ſo Sacred, and their Authority is thus wholly from God, how is it ſaid in the holy Scriptures that ſome of the Kings even now mentioned were made by the people, and ſo received their Regal power from them, and by their Election ?* Is it not ſaid of Saul,

(h) 2 Sam. 11. (h) that all the people went to *Gilgal,* and there made
15. him King before the Lord ? Of David, (i) the men of *Ju-*
(i) 2 Sam. 5. *dah* anointed *David* king of *Judah,* the Elders of *Iſrael* anointed *David* king over *Iſrael?*

Theod.

Theodidactus. [k] *Zadek* the Prieſt and *Nathan* the Pro- [k 1 King 1.]
phet anointed *Solomon* King, and the Lord alſo anointed
him, otherwiſe he had not been the Lords anointed, but the
anointed of *Zadok* and *Nathan.* The Lord anointed *Solo-*
mon as Maſter of the ſubſtance, and gave unto him his Regal power; *Zadok* and *Nathan* anointed *Solomon,* as Maſter
of the ceremony, and declared that God had given unto
him this power. For outward unction doth not confer up-
on Kings their authority (when without it [l] *Cyrus,* and [l Eſay. 45.]
before the uſe thereof ſome of the [m] Patriarchs o- [m 1 Chro. 16.]
ver their families were the anointed of the Lord), but it is
a ſign only of Sovereignty, becauſe if we poure oyl into the
ſame veſſel with any other liquor, it wil be alway uppermoſt.

The Elders then of *Judah* and *Iſrael* [n] anointing *Da-* [n 2 Sam. 2.]
vid King, did manifeſt him to be their King ; but did not
give unto him the right unto his Kingdom, this was only [o 1 Sam. 16.]
from the [o] Lords appointing. [2 Sam. 5.]

In like manner *Saul* firſt [p] *anointed by the Lord to be* [p 1 Sam. 10.]
Captain over his Inheritance, upon the Petition of the people [q] *ſet a King over them by the Lord,* and choſen im- [q Ibid.]
mediately by God to be a King, as [r] *Matthias* was to be [r Act. 1.]
an Apoſtle by *caſting lots* ; *God made him King* ; he only
gave unto him Kingly power, and not the people : who [ſ 1 Sam. 10.]
notwithſtanding after all this, are ſaid to *make him King*
by approving him as made by God, and receiving him in- *Conſtituere regem,*
to the poſſeſſion of his Kingdom to exerciſe his Regal au- *eſt verbum tota*
thority, whom the ſons of *Belial* had rejected. The peo- *conjugatione, quod*
ple *then made Saul King,* not by giving unto him the right *cum eſſeret ampli-*
of his Kingdom, but by putting him into the poſſeſſion of *cere actionem pro-*
his Kingdom to reign over them : For the Jewes by Gods *regnare eſt regnum*
ſpecial [t] commandement being to make ſuch a one King, *exercere poteſta-*
whom their Lord God had choſen, unto whom their Lord *tem; quaſi diceret,*
God had given Regal Authority ; from their Lord God, *facerent, ut regiam*
and not from themſelves, from heaven and not from earth, *poteſtatem exerce-*
was the Soveraignty of their Princes. [t Deut. 17.]

For as in the Spiritual Graces which God mercifully be-
ſtoweth upon the faithful, neither the outward miniſtry of
Paul in planting, nor of *Apollo in watring,* is any thing, but

u 1 Cor. 3.
u *God giveth the encrease*: So in the civil power which God vouchfafeth untoPrinces,the people are not *any thing* in regard of giving this Authority, but God only is the free Donor thereof.

Philale. Although the power of Princes is not from the people ; yet it is often derived unto them from their noble Progenitors by fucceffion, or obtained through their own prowefle; and by lawful conqueft : how then is it onely, and immediately from God ?

Theodidaɫtus. Succeffion, and lawful conqueft,are Titles whereby Princes receive their Authority, they are not the original, and immediate fountain of this Authority. Heat, moifture, cold, drinefs, and our temper arifing from them (whiles we are miraculoufly fafhioned in our mothers womb) are preparations whereby our bodies are made fit receptacles for our fouls ; but the y Creator of our foul is God : So Princes have juft claim unto their Sovereign power by the titles of fucceffion & conqueft; but the prime Author of their power is God. *Inde illis eft poteftas* (faith z *Tertullian*) *unde fpiritus* : thence have they their power whence their fpirit. And before him a *Irenæus: Cujus juffu nafcuntur homines, ejus juffu conftituuntur Principes*: By whofe appointment they are born men and made reafonable creatures (and that is by God only who b infufeth into them their foul by creating it) by his appointment are they made Princes. And as they receive their power only from God, fo for the good or evil adminiftration thereof, they are accountable only unto God,as unto their Superiour, and not unto any mortal creature. God only maketh them Kings, and God only can unmake them, and dejeɫt them from their Thrones.

y Ecclef. 12.

z Apologet.c.30.
a Lib. 5. cont.
Hær.

b Lombard.l.2.
Sentent.diftinɫt.
17.

Philalethes. Were not the Priefts amongft the Jewes Superiours unto their Kings to judge, and dethrone them, if they were delinquent ?

*Theodidaɫtus.*No,rather Priefts were fubjeɫt unto Kings, and punifhed by them for their offences. c *Abimelek* the Prieft acknowledged himfelf King *Sauls* fervant. *Let not the King impute any thing unto his fervant,*faith *Abimelek,* fpeaking

c 1 Sam. 12.

speaking of himſelf. And again unto King *Saul: thy ſervant knew nothing of this.* And leſt it might be thought that theſe words were uttered by a timerous ſpirit, unto *Saul* a [d] Tyrant; *David* a religious [e] Prince calleth *Zadok* the Prieſt his ſervant. Neither was *Solomon* behind *David* his father in the knowledg of his Sovereign authority over Prieſts, when he depoſed *Abiathar* the high Prieſt, and placed *Zadok* in his room.

Philalethes. Indeed the [f] text ſaith, Solomon *caſt out Abiathar from being a Prieſt unto the Lord*: but ſome attribute this fact of depoſition unto *Solomon* as he was a Prophet: becauſe it immediatly followeth in the ſame text, that he might fulfil the words of the Lord againſt the houſe of *Ely.*

Theodidactus. The fulfilling of this propheſie was not the motive that excited *Solomon* to depoſe *Abiathar*, but *Abiathars* [g] conſpiracy and treaſon with *Adonijah*: for the words, *that he might fulfil,* &c, do not ſhew the cauſe why *Solomon* did caſt out *Abiathar*, but the conſequent of this fact; which was foretold by a Prophet, but not accompliſhed by *Solomon* as a Prophet. Men foretel things to come as Prophets, they do not put the things foretold in execution as Prophets: For then the [h] ſoldiers were Prophets caſting lots upon Chriſts garment, *that the Scripture might be fulfilled;* [i] *Herod* was a Prophet fulfilling the propheſie of *Jeremie,* by murthering the *Innocents.* And many other inſtances might be given in this kinde, which I paſs over, becauſe the main point which occaſioneth the producing of them, the ſubjection of Prieſts among the Jewes unto their Kings, is ingeniouſly acknowledged by ſome of the Jeſuits. In the Old Teſtament (ſaith [k] one of the firſt and chiefeſt of that ſeditious order; *under the Law of Nature, or of Moſes, Prieſts were ſubject unto Kings.*

Philalethes. I have heard of other Romaniſts that have exalted the Jewiſh high Prieſts above the Thrones of Kings, and that do alledge unto this purpoſe ſome particular examples: As of the high Prieſt [l] *Azari*, who with fourſcore other Prieſts [m] valiantly aſſailed King *Oziah* ſtricken

Marginal notes:
[d] 1 King. 1.
[e] 1 King. 2.
[f] 1 King 2.
[g] 1 King. c.1, 2
[h] John 19.
[i] Matth. 2.
[k] *Salmer. t act.*
[k] 3 *de poteſtate eccleſiaſt & ſecul.*
[l] 2 Chron. 26.
[m] *Allen. defen. Eng. Cath. c. 5.*

with

n *Allen. ibid.*
o *Levit. 13.*
x *Auctoritate regnandi. Bellarm. lib. 5. de Pont Rom. c. 8.*
p 2 *King 11.*
* *Fovet et cultum Baal. Bellarm. l. 5. de Pont. c. 8.*

with the leprosie, for burning Incense unto the Lord; n did thrust him by force out of the Temple ; according to the Levitical o Law against Lepers, constrained him to go or of the City, and deprived him * of his Kingly Authoriti. Of p *Jehoida,* who being chief Priest, caused Queen *Athalia* to be slain, because she * maintained the Idolatrous worship of *Baal,* and made *Joas* King in her stead.

q 2 Chro. 26. 20.

r Ibid.
* *Antiquitet. Judaic. l. 9. c. 11.*
whom *Cajetan* doth follow upon the 2 *Chro. 26.* visâ *lepra Sacerdotes Regem leprosum ad festinè egrediendum morent*
* *De verb. Isaia vid. Dom. Ho. 4.*
f 2 King. 15.
* *Joseph lib. 9. Antiq. cap. 11.*
1 2 Kings 15.
u Levit. 13.
x 2 Chro. 26. 21
y Ibid. ver. 23.

Theodidactus. These facts of *Azaria* & *Jehoida,* if they were sincerely related out of the Book of God, they would make little for the superiority of Priests over Kings: For first the Scripture saith not that *Azaria* violently assailed *Ozia,* or did by force thrust him out of the Temple: he was q compelled (without any force from *Azariah*) by the immediate hand of God, striking him with leprosie, to go out thence. And when it is said r *Azariah* the chief Priest with others caused *Ozia* hastily to depart from the Temple, this (as * *Josephus* doth testifie) was only by words and admonition. And x *Chrysostome* giveth the reason, *For the office of a Priest is only to reprove, and freely to admonish, not to move arms, nor to use bucklers, nor to shake a launce, neither to bend a bowe, nor to shoot forth darts, but onely to argue and freely to admonish.*
Neither did *Azaria* deprive *Ozia* of his Kingly authority, which he held unto his death: for he was f sixteen years old when he was made King, raigned two and fifty years, and * died being threescore and eight years old. And although by reason of his Leprosie t dwelling apart according unto the prescript of the u Law, his Son *Jotham* was his vicegerent to x rule the Kings house and the people of the Land : yet until *Ozia y was buried with his Fathers Jotham raigned not in his stead,* he had not the right of the Kingdome.

Philalethes. You have given a sufficient answer unto this example of *Azaria* ; but the other of *Jehoida* seemeth to have more difficulty.

Theodidactus. In this instance likewise I shall, I trust, easily give you satisfaction, if you will but call unto mind, first

2 2 Kings 8.
a 2 Kings 9.
b 2 Kings 11.

how *Ahazia* z son of *Joram,* and a King of *Judah,* dying, his mother b *Athalia slew all the Kings seed save Joas* the son of

of *Ahazia*, whom c *Jehoshcba* his Aunt, and Wife unto *Je-* c 2 King.11.12.
hoida the high Prieſt *had ſtollen from among the Kings Sons*
that ſhould be ſlain, and hid him in the houſe of the Lord
ſix years.

Secondly, That *Jehoida* not as high Prieſt, but as *Joas's*
Uncle by marriage, and a Protector over him by reaſon of
this alliance ; and *not alone, but* d *with the Captains of hun-* d 2 Chror.23.
dreds, with the Levites out of all Cities, and with the chief
fathers of Iſrael, brought forth Joas *King* Ahazias *ſon*, did
put upon him the Crown, and declared him to be King
who was rightfully ſo, both by the title of ſucceſſion , and e 2 Chron 23.
e Gods own ſpecial appointment. · 11.

f Thirdly, After they had thus ſeated *Joas* in his Regal f 2 Chron. 3.
Throne, by his authority, *Jehoida* commanded *Athalia* as 14. 15.
a bloody Uſurper of the Kingdom to be ſlain, ſo that indeed *Joas* the true heir of the Scepter of *Judah*, and not
Jehoida the Prieſt, puniſhed *Athalia* uſurping the Crown.

Philalethes. I do now plainly perceive that ſuch as endeavour to advance the Miter above the Crown, the Prieſt-
hood above Regal power, have no ground hereof in the
Old Teſtament : yet peradventure out of the New Teſtament they may alledge ſomwhat for this prepoſterous ſub-
ordination

Theodidactus. If Kings before the coming of Chriſt had
ſupream Authority over Prieſts and all ſorts of men within
the circuit of their juriſdictions: Chriſt ſince hath not di-
miniſhed, or embaſed this Soveraignty. *Audite Judai, &*
Gentes. (ſaith Saint x *Auguſtine* ſpeaking in the perſon of * Tractat.t1 5.
in Johannem.
his Saviour) *audi circumciſio, audi praputium, audite regna*
terrena, &c. Hearken ye Jewes, hearken ye Gentiles, hearken Circumciſion, hearken uncircumciſion, hear all earth-
ly Kingdoms ; I do not hinder your ruling and reigning in
this world, *My Kingdom is not of this World*, it is heavenly and ſpiritual. And therefore g Chriſt hath not made g Hom 23 na.
Laws to overthrow policies and States, but for the better 15 21 X m.
ordering and eſtabliſhing of them.

Is not this one of his inviolable decrees promulgated by *
his *

his elect Servant and Apostle [b] Saint *Paul*: *Let every soul be subject unto the higher powers.*

Philalethes. What higher powers?

Theodidactus. Such as bear the sword, to whom tribute is due. And hence [*] *Augustine, Chrysostome,* [*] and almost all the ancients, have understood *Paul* to speak, *tantùm*, only of secular powers?

Philalethes. Who are subject unto these higher secular powers?

Theodidactus. Every soul, [*] although an Apostle, an Evangelist, a Prophet, whosoever he be. This the Apostle St. *Paul* himself did testifie in his own person, who [i] stood at *Cæsars* judgment, where (saith he) ἐδεῖ κρίνεσθαι I ought to be judged, unto whose sentence out of dutie I am to submit my selfe.

And no marvel if Saint *Paul* acknowledged himself subject unto *Cæsar,* when his Master Christ paid unto him tribute, and confessed one of *Cæsars* subordinate Magistrates, [k] *Pilate* to have power over him, and that given from above.

Our eternall [l] high Priest, as man, thus humbling himself under the command of civil powers; his chief Disciple Saint *Peter* also writeth unto his *fellow Presbyters,* whom hee exhorteth [m] *to feed the flock of God,* that they would submit themselves unto the [n] *King as unto the Superiour.*

Philalethes. These two exhortations of Saint *Peter,* that his-*fellow Presbyters* would *feed the flock of God,* and also *submit themselves unto Kings,* seem to be repugnant one to the other; For Kings that have given their names to Christ are sheep of *Gods* fold, and so to [o] obey their spirituall Pastors *having over-sight of them.* And if Kings are to obey their spirituall Pastors, how are spirituall Pastors subject unto Kings.

Theodidactus. [p] All the tribes of *Israel* (and therefore the tribe of *Levi* and the Priests) witnessed that the Lord had said to *David* thou shalt feed my people *Israel.* And King

(marginal notes:)
[b] Rom. 13.
[*] *Jesuits Parer. disputat. 10. nu. 13 ad Rom.* [*] *At que omnes ferè veteres.*
[*] *Chrys. st. in 13. ad Roman. with whom Theodor. Theophil. Oecumen. do accord.* [i] Act. 25.
[k] John 19.
[l] Heb.
[m] 1 Pet. 5. 2.
[n] 1 Pet. 2. 15.
Heb. 13.

King *David* himfelf calleth them his q fheep : Kings then q 1 Sam. 14.
are alfo Paftors, and all within their dominions, even *David cum An-*
Priefts themfelvs are fheep of their fold. *gelum vidiſſet*
percutientem in

 Philalethes. This inftance doth not fatisfie the doubt *plebem, ait ego*
I moved, but rather doth ftrengthen it : for how can *peccavi, & ego*
Kings and Priefts be mutually Paftors one to ano- *paſtor malignus*
ther ? *feci, & hic grex*
quid fecit? Am-

 Theodidaktus. After a divers manner. A *Paſtor*, or Shep- *broſ. Epiſt 28.*
herd (faith r *Chryſoſtome*) *may with great authority enforce* r Lib 2. de Sa-
his ſheep to ſuffer the curing of their wounds when they are *cerd.*
not willing hereunto, and may compel them to keep in fertile
and fafe paſtures, if they go aſtray and feed in barren places.
Such kind of Paftors by a borrowed fpeech are Kings, who
may command their Subjects by the terrour, and compul-
fion of corporal punifhments. But *Biſhops* or *Prieſts* (as the
fame f *Chryſoſtome* fpeaketh) *are to move men by perfwaſion* f Ibid.
fpiritually to be *cured, and not by offering* ` *violence, as Lords* t 1 Pet 5.3.
over Gods heritage.

 As therefore all the faithful are to u *ſubmit themſelvs one* u 1 Pet. 5.5.
to another, in Chriftian reproofs, and admonitions; So Princes are to be obedient unto fpiritual Paftors, befeeching
them as Embaffadors from Chrift, and delivering unto
them his heavenly meffage. And if Princes by this meffage
learning what is acceptable unto God, fhall by their Authority enjoyn it publickly to be embraced, they may enforce the fame fpiritual Paftors to obey his command by
temporal chaftifements.

 A Prince failing unto fome forraign Port in his own fhip,
and guided by his own Subjects, in this maritime paffage
he fubmitteth himfelf unto the conduct and direction of
the Pilot ; whom notwithftanding, if he wilfully erreth in
the performance of his duty, he may feverely punifh with
lofs of liberty, goods, or life : So Princes in the Church,
which the Antients have refembled unto a fhip, walking
towards the Port of Heaven, they are to hearken unto the
meaneft of Gods fervants, fincerely declaring unto them
the facred will of God; yet if they fhall publifh rather their
own

own errours than Gods truth, or otherwife offend, Princes may correct and punifh them, and they are patiently to o-bey.

Princes then owe obedience unto Gods direction uttered by his Embaſſadors for the ſalvation of their souls, by reaſon of which pretious benefit x ordina-rily attending their Miniſtry, *Nothing* (ſaith x *Am-broſe*) *is more excellent, nothing more ſublime than a Biſhop.* And again, Gods Miniſters owe obed:-ence unto Princes, and are ſubject unto their co-ercive puniſhments; who are free from all puniſhmencs that man may inflict. In which reſpect * *Tertul-lian* in the name of all the Chriſtians in his daies, ſaith, *We honour the Emperour in ſuch ſort as is lawful for us, and expedient for them as a man next unto God, and obtaining from God whatſoever he hath, and only inferiour unto God.*

Philalethes. Did any other Fathers of the primitive Church acknowledg this eminent Soveréignty in the Em-perors of thoſe times.

Theodidactus. As many as had occaſion to write hereof. * *Optatus* ſaith: *There is not any man above the Emperour.* * *Chryſoſtome* ſaith of the Emperour *Theodoſius: He had no man equal unto him upon earth,* he was *the top and head of all men upon earth.* y *Cyril* writeth unto *Theodoſius* the yonger: *Veſtræ ſerenitati, unto your Excellencie there is no ſtate equal,* much leſſe ſuperiour. z *Agapetus* affirm-eth of the Emperour *Juſtinian, He hath a higher dignity than any man: he hath not upon Earth any higher than himſelf.*

Philalethes. If the antient Fathers of ſuch different times (for between *Optatus* and *Agapetus* there were neer two hundred years) almoſt in the ſame phraſe of ſpeech ſo extolled the dignity of the Emperour; when did the Biſhop of *Rome* challenge his pretended eminency above the Emperour ?

margin notes:
x Jo 20.
* De dignitat. Sacerd.cap.3.

* ad Scapulam.

* Lib. 3.
*Hom.2.ad pop. Antioch.
y Praefat. lib. adverſ. Julian.
z In para. neſ: nu.3.& nu.21.

Theodi-

Theodidactus. Not five hundred years after Chrift: For then *Pelagius* the firft Roman Bifhop of that name thus writeth unto *Childebert* King of *France* : ' *With how great ftudy and labour are we to ftrive, that for removing the fcandal of fufpition, we may minifter the obfequioufnefs of our confeffion unto* KINGS, *unto whom the holy Scripture commandeth us to be fubject.* Neither fix hundred years after Chrift *:* for about that time *ᵇ Gregory the great, likewife Bifhop of* Rome, *religioufly confeffed, that power was given from above unto the Emperour above all men.* And then reckoning himfelf in this number of *all men,* ᶜ addeth, *I being fubject unto your command,* not out of fained humility, but out of confcience and duty, *on both parts have payed what* ᵈ *I ought, becaufe I have* yielded *obedience unto the Emperour, and not holden my peace in what I thought for God.* Nay, nine hundred years from Chrift, the Bifhops of *Rome* were in fuch fubjection unto the Emperours, that even in that age the Emperours punifhed them with the deprivation of their Bifhopricks, if they were criminous', as *Otho* the Emperour depofed *John* the 22. for his impure and vitious life.

· Philalethes. *At what time then did the Bifhop of* Rome *firft fo far exalt himfelf above the Emperours, as to prefume to deprive them of their imperial Crowns, and depofe them from their Thrones ?*

Theodidactus. More then a thoufand years from the Afcenfion of our bleffed Saviour. *Gregory* the feventh, otherwife called *Hildebrand*, chofen Bifhop of *Rome* ᵉ about the year of our Lord 1073. was the firft that did attempt this prophane and fcandalous outrage againft the Emperour *Henry the fourth.*

· I read *and read again (* faith ᶠ *Otho Frifingenfis* an Hiftorian, living near the times of *Hildebrand) the geftes of the Roman Kings and Emperours ,* and ᵍ *nowhere I find any of them, before this man (* Henry the fourth *) excommunicated by the Bifhop of* Rome, *or deprived of his kingdom.* And the ill fuccefs of the chief *Actors* in this furious *attempt* of depofing this Emperour, might well have difcouraged

the

E

a Epift 16 *ad Childeb. tom.* 2 *Concil.*

b L'l: 2 *Epift: Epift:* 61.

c Ego juſſioni ſubjectus.

d Quod debui.

e Bellar. in Chron.

f Lego & relego. Lib 6. *cap.* 35. *g Nuſquam reverio quemquam ante hunc.*

the Bishops of *Rome* in succeeding ages to meddle again
with such ungodly enterprises. *Rodolph* Duke of *Swevia*
whom (at the instigation of *Gregory* the seventh) some
of the Princes of *Germany* had set up to take the Empire
from *Henry* the fourth by force of armes, in fighting a-
gainst this Emperour he lost his right hand: and when,
by reason of that and other wounds, he was ready to
breath out his distressed soul, *looking on the stump of his
arm, and fetching a deep sigh, he said unto the Bishops that
were about him, Behold this is the hand wherewith I did swear
allegiancee to my Soveraign Lord* Henry. And Pope *Hildebrand* himself (whiles he was in contention with the
same Emperour, to depose him) by the consent of his
own people the Romans, *was deprived of his Popedome*;
and afterwards lying at the point of death, *he called
unto him one of the twelve Cardinals, whom he loved above the
rest, and confessed unto God, Saint* Peter, *and the whole
Church, that he had greatly sinned in the Pastoral charge
which was committed unto him, and that at the instinct of the
Devil he had stirred hatred and heart-burning amongst men.*
For *Hildebrands* deposing of *Henry* the fourth, was like
the *Violence of a tempest, which stirred up so many ca-
lamities, so many schismes, so many perils of bodies and
souls, that it alone* (saith *Otho* ᵈ *Frisengensis*) *through
the fierceness and continuance thereof, may sufficiently prove
the greatness of mans misery.*

Philalethes. *Two most remarkable examples! they do
clearly illustrate that speech of the Wise-man,* Take not part
with the seditious;*for who knoweth the ruine of them
both? But all this while you have declared only the truth of
the first principle of* Kingly Soveraignty *in his excellent
Majesty; That receiving authority immediately from*
GOD, *he hath no Superiour to punish him or chastise
him, but GOD alone. I would therefore now intreat you to
take the same paines in establishing the second principle of his
supreme power; The bond of his Subjects, in obedience
unto his Majesty, is inviolable, and cannot be dissolved.*

Theodidactus

*a Vespergens.
Anni 1080.*

*b Sigeb. Anni
1084
c Sigeb. anni
1085
Found this
written of him.*

*d Chro. lib. 6
cap. 36*

Theodidactus. The principal meanes, whereby the seditious sons of *Belial* do pretend that this *sacred bond* may be dissolved, are either supposed crimes in the persons of Princes, *as Tyranny in governing, Infidelity, Heresie, Apostacy*; or Episcopal acts of the Bishop of *Rome, as his Dispensations, and Excommunications.*

Philalethes. *How do you prove, that Tyranny in government doth not unloose this bond?*

Theodidactus. Was not *Saul* a Tyrant, *in hunting after the soul, and* seeking the life of *David, who was most* faithful unto him amongst all his servants, whom he himself confessed to *have rendred unto him good for evil?*

Was he not a bloody oppressor, in commanding *Doeg,* without any just cause of offence, violently to run upon *the Priests, and to slay fourscore and five persons that did wear a Linnen Ephod; to smite* Nob *the City of the Priests, both Man and Woman, both Childe and Suckling, both Oxe, Asse, and Sheep, with the edge of the sword?*

The blood of so many Innocents did cry unto GOD for vengeance, and by his special Commandement (*Who so sheddeth mans blood, by man his blood shall be shed*) deserved death: yet *David,* not an ordinary or private man, but by GODS own appointment designed unto the Kingdome, a chief Captain and Leader in the Kings battels, the Kings Son in law, when he had *Saul* delivered into his hands, and was encouraged by his servants to destroy him, said unto them, *The Lord keep me from doing that thing unto my Master the Lords annointed, to lay my hand upon him; for he is the Lords annointed:* And after unto *Saul* himself; *Wickedness proceedeth from the wicked, but mine hand shall not be upon thee:* and again unto *Abishai,* when the Lord another time had closed Saul into his hand; *Destroy him not, for who can lay hands upon the Lords anointed, and be guiltless?* Which Pious and Religious acts of *David towards* Saul, amongst the *Israelites,* Optatus hath elegantly described, the

E 2   more

a 1 Sam 14 13
b 1 Sam. 22. 23
c 1 Sam. 22. 13
d 1 Sam. 24 17

e 1 Sam. 22. 18, 19

f Gen 9 6

g 1 Sam. 24. 6

h Verse 14

i 1 Sam. 26. 9

more effectually to commend them unto Christians. David (faith [a] *Optatus*) *had the occasion of victory in his hands, he might have cut the throat of his unwary and secure adversary, without any labour : he might without shedding of blood, without any conflict, have changed a publick war into a private slaughter. And his men, the victory, occasion, and opportunity encouraged him ; he began to draw his sword, his armed hand was moving towards the throat of his enemy ; but the perfect remembrance of* GODS *Commandements stayed him : he withstanding his men, and the occasions inciting him, in effect thus speaketh unto them : O victory, thou dost in vain provoke and invite me with thy triumphs : I would willingly conquer mine enemy; but I must rather keep Gods Commandements. I will not (faith he) lay my hands upon the Lords annointed. And so he repressed his hand together with his sword : and whiles he feared the oyl, saved his enemy.*

Philalethes. Our blessed Saviours own precept and commandement is clear enough for the preserving of the lives, or of any thing else belonging to our enemies : Love [b] *(faith he) your enemies, blesse them that curse you, do good to them that hate you, and pray for them that hurt you, and persecute you.*

Theodidactus. You say well, that these words are CHRISTS *precept* or *commandement :* our Saviours preface unto them ('Εγὼ λέγω ὑμῖν,) I fay unto you, it is my decree) do h sufficiently prove it ; and the words immediately following them (*that you may be the Children of your Father which is in Heaven*) are a most forcible motive to stir us up readily, and with alacrity to yield obedience unto this commandement. Although then Kings and Princes, through their tyranny, persecution, and oppression, shou'd be our enemies, as *Saul* was unto *David* (thine [c] enemy, faith *Abishai* of *Saul* unto *David,*) yet we are to love [d] them from our hearts, to blesse and pray for them with our tongues, and to do good unto them by our actions. For these duties by our Saviours commandement are to be performed of us unto private men that are our enemies ; much more.

unto

a l. b 2 adv rf.
p.7.n.

b Mat. 5.

c 1 Sam. 24.
d Salvator tria
praecipit inimicis
erit. benda : quorum primum diligere ad Cor periunt ; secundum nempe benefacere ad opw ;tertium benedicere, 1. bene precari & orare, ad linguam. Jansenins. cap. 40.
Con.

unto publick perfons,the Princes and Potentates of the
Earth. That elect veffel Saint *Paul* exhorting us to
bleffe all men by our prayers, fupplications, and interceffions,
prefently mentioneth *Kings, and all that are in authority,*
as perfons for whom, after a more fpecial manner, we
are to pour out our fupplications unto God. Likewife
Tertullian teaching, that according unto the Chriftian
doctrine,*To wifh evil,to do evil, to think evil,is indifferent-*
ly forbidden us towards all men, thence inferreth, if we
are not to offer the leaft of thefe injuries to *any man,*
much leffe to him that is fo highly advanced by our GOD,
fpeaking of the Emperour.

Philalethes. *Who was this Emperour,of whom* Tertullian *fpeaketh?*

Theodidactus. It was *Severus:* for under him (faith
Hierem) *Tertullian* flourifhed.

Philalethes. *Was this Emperour a Tyrant in his go-*
vernment?

Theodidactus. Yea,an unbelieving Tyrant, an Infidel,
that did grievoufly perfecute the Chriftians, whom he
did affliCt *with the fifth famous perfecution.*

Philalethes. *Then I perceive by* Tertullians *judgement,*
that not only tyranny, but likewife tyranny joyned with infi-
delity, doth not unloofe the bond of duty and obedience from
Subjects unto their Soveraign.

Theodidactus. You may learn this truth from a more
ancient and authentick Author then *Tertullian,* even
from the bleffed Apoftle Saint *Peter:* This holy Servant
of GOD writ his firft Epiftle in the *time of* Claudius
the Emperour, and did direCt it unto his Countrymen
the Jews, *here and there throughout Pontus, Galatia ,Cap-*
padocia, Afia, Bythinia, which were Regions then fubjeCt
unto the Roman Emperour. For many yeares before
Claudius raign, *Pompey* the great made thefe Regions Roman Provinces.

And becaufe fome Seducers(as *Jofephus* witneffeth)
had perfivaded the Jews,under a pretext of maintain-
ing their liberty, that tribute was not to be paid to

E 3 *Cefar,*

a 1 Tim. 2.

b In *Apologetico*
cap 36.

c In *Catal.*

d *Severus quintus*
poft Neronem per-
fecutione Chriftia-
nos excruciavit;
OROS. & BA-
RO: anCHR:
205. *Sæviffima*
perfecutione.
Baro. to 1 anno
45
e *The Remifls in*
their table of Pe-
ter.
f 1 Pet. 1
g S^rgm: *Com-*
ment: in l b: 1
Sulpitii.
h *Judaicarum*
Antiquit: lib: 18
cap: 1 & lib: 2
de bello Judaico:
cap: 12.

Cæsar, neither any *mortal man* was to be accounted as a Prince or Lord over them, but GOD only : Saint *Peter* exhorteth them so to be *free*, *as not having their liberty for a cloak of maliciousness*, but as *the servants of GOD*, and to *fear GOD*, but yet *to honour the King also* : And although Magistrates be men, and so their *ordinance*, in regard of the persons in whom it doth reside, but *humane* : yet *to submit themselves unto* them, *for the Lords sake*, from whom they received their authority.

a 1 Peter 2. 16 & 18

Philalethes. *This* King, *whom Saint* Peter *would have his brethren the Jews to honour, and that as Supreme, cannot be any other then the Emperour* Claudius, *under whom* (*as you have shewed*) Saint Peter *writ his Epistle* , *and whose Subjects were the inhabitants of* Pontus, Galatia , Cappadocia, Asia, Bythinia, *unto whom Saint* Peter *inscribed his Epistle. And Saint* Peter *might well term this Emperour a King, because the* Roman Emperours *(saith* Appian *) were in all their deeds and actions* Kings.

Præf. Hist.

Theodidactus. Your collection and inference is very firm, and full of truth : And therefore Saint *Peter* exhorteth his brethren the Jews (himself residing then at *Rome*) *to submitt themselves ; and to be subject unto a profane* Infidel, a cruel Tyrant. For *Claudius*, upon the sight of the least prodigy, worshipped the heathen gods after the custome of the ancient Romans : he was *naturally* so mercilefs, and given to *blood-shed*, that he would have *tortures in examinations, punishments for Parricides* executed in his *own presence* : he had most *cruel searchers* of all that came but to salute him, sparing not any *Sex* or *Age*; delighted to see the faces of *Fencers* (whose throats he had caused to be cut, for stumbling by chance in their sword-fights) *as they lay gasping and yeilding up their breath*: he was excessively *given to the wanton love of women*, *and was* so *inthralled unto his wives and. freemen, that, as it was commodious unto them or stood with their affection, he granted honourable Dignities, conferred*

b Baro. anno 45 Rhemists in their table of Peter
c Suet. cap. 22
d Suet. cap. 34

e Suet. cap. 33
f Suet. cap. 29

the

the conducts of armies, and decreed impunities or punishments.

Unto such an unbelieving and bloody oppressor,
Saint *Peter* earnestly exhorteth the believing Jews to
yield obedience.

*Philalethes. After what manner ? In outward shew and
appearance, only of constraint, and because (willed they,
nilled they) they were to obey ?*

Theodidactus. No: for Saint *Paul* writing his Epistle
unto the Romans 'living under the same Emperour,
commandeth *every soul to be subject unto the higher powers,* and *not because of wrath,* not out of fear of outward
force, or violence, *but for conscience sake* ; and for that
these higher powers are the *Ordinance of GOD, the Mi-
nisters of GOD.* And this is, as the same Apostle else-
where *admonisheth,* to yield obedience unto them
from the heart, as serving the Lord and not men.

Which heavenly doctrine of the Apostles was afte-
ward often iterated by the Fathers of the Primitive
Church in their Writings, least by the fraud of Satan
it might slip out of the minds of th faithful. *Justin
Martyr,* in the name of the Christians in his dayes,
saith unto *Antoninus,* an unbelieving Emperour, and
a persecutor; *We only adore GOD, and in all other
things (not of constraint but) cheerfully perform service unto you:* And *Augustine : The powers that are, are
of GOD: hence we honour a Gentile placed in power,
although he himself,* who holding Gods Order giveth thanks unto the Devil, *be unworthy : for the
power requireth it, and deserveth honour,* as ordained of
GOD.

*Philalethes. Howsoever Infidelity doth not dissolve the
bond of a Subject in duty and allegiance unto his Soveraign;
yet may not Heresie and Apostacy ?*

*Theodidactus. Constantius, Valens, Valentinia-
nus* the younger, were Arian Hereticks: yet we
read not that they were rejected by Orthodox
Christians as unlawful, and usurping Emperours.
And

a *Rhemists in
their table of
Paul.*
b *Rom.* 13

c *Col.* 3.
Ephes. 6

d *Persecutio* 4.
sub Antonino.
Euseb. in Chron.
c *Apol.* 2. ad
Antoni. Imper.

And (which is worſe) *was not* Julian an Apoſtate, *an Ido-*
later?)et [a]*Chriſtian Souldiers ſerved this unbelieving Lord;*
and when he ſaid, Go forth to fight, invade ſuch a Nation,
they obeyed.

Phi'alethes. *Some ſay this was for want of ſtrength and*
forces to reſiſt.

Theodidactus. They could not want ſtrength, when
the greateſt part of *Julians* Army were Chriſtians, as it
appeared inſtantly upon his death, by their joynt excla-
mation unto *Jovinian* his Succeſſor:For this Army chu-
ſing *Jovinian* Emperour, and he refuſing to have any
Imperial command over them, becauſe he was a Chriſtian,and they Pagans, [b] *all of them with one voice made an-*
ſwer And we are Chriſtians. It was not then for want of
power they obeyed,but rather,as [c] *Auguſtine* writeth of
them, *They were ſubject unto* Julian *their temporal Lord, for*
his ſake that was their eternal Lord and Maſter, and out of
obedience unto his commandements.

If Subjects are obliged in duty,and out of conſcience,
cheerfully to obey *tyrannous, unbelieving, heretical, apoſta-*
tical Princes,as *Powers ordained of God*, with what alacrity then ſhould we be in all things obſequious unto our
gracious and religious Soveraign ? *Gracious,* as being like
unto GOD, whoſe Vicegerent he is in this,that his clemency and mercy *is over all his works* : *Religious,* in that
he is a zealous propugner of the ancient and Catholick
Faith,not only by his Kingly power and authority, but
likewiſe by the *learned pen of a ready Writer.*

Notwithſtanding ſome are ſo blinded with the Roman ſuperſtition, that they are ready upon ſome pretended acts of the Biſhop of *Rome,* as upon his *Diſpenſa-*
tions, or Excommunications, to renounce their obedience
unto ſo merciful and pious a Prince.

Philalethes. *May not then the Biſhop of* Rome, *either*
by diſpenſing with the law, which bindeth Subjects unto obe-
dience ; or with the Oath,whereby they ſincerely ſwear to per-
form this obedience unto his excellent Majeſty, unlooſe the bond
of their allegiance ?

Theodidactus.

a Aug. 124 Iſ.

b Ruſſia. lib. 2.
hiſt. cap. 1

c In Pſal. 124.

Theodidactus. The Bishop of *Rome* cannot dispense
with the Law of Nature ; which *from the first begin-* a *Aquin.* 1.2.
ning of the reasonable creature is unchangeable, nor with *q. 94. Art.5.*
the Moral Law of G O D, *whose Precepts are in-* b *1.2. q.100.*
dispensable. But the duty of Subjects in obedience unto *Art. 8.*
their Soveraign, is grounded upon the Law of Nature ;
beginning with our first beginning. For as we be born
Sons, so we are born *Subjects* : his *Sons*, from whose
loyns ; his *Subjects*, in whose Dominions we are born.
The same duties of Subjects are also enjoyned by the
Moral Law, and particularly (as you shewed in the
very entrance unto this our Conference) in the fifth
Commandment, *Honor thy Father and thy Mother* : where,
as we are required to honor the *Fathers* of private Families, so much more the *Father* of our Countrey and
the whole Kingdom. And as the Bishop of *Rome* cannot dispense with these Laws imposing upon us Obedience unto His M A J E S T Y, so neither with the
Oath we take to persevere in this Obedience. When
David said, *I have sworn that I will keep thy righteous* c *Psal.* 119.
Judgements, if the Bishop of *Rome* had been then in his
fulnefs of power, could he have dispensed with this
Oath ? And so if any now, by the example of *David*,
swear to keep Gods righteous Judgements of *not com-
mitting Adultery*, or of *honoring their Parents, and Magistrates* ; he cannot free them from this Oath : but if we
violate both these Commandments, we are as well *Re-
bels*, as *Adulterers.*

Philalethes. *Are not the Excommunications of the Bishop
of Rome of more force to loose the bond of Allegiance, than his
Dispensations ?*

Theodidactus. These likewise have no power to work
this effect. Excommunication upon a contempt unto
the Church, doth not make a man worse than an d *Eth-* d *Mat.* 18.
nick : but you have heard that both Saint *Peter* and Saint
Paul, earnestly exhort us to be subject unto Heathen,
F   and

and Ethnick Princes ; and therefore we may also yield obedience unto excommunicated Princes : besides, Excommunication (according to the doctrine of the [*] Romanists themselves) doth not free a servant from obedience unto his Master, or a son unto his Father. And Kings are as *Masters*, and *Subjects* as *Servants*; for so *David* calleth *Saul* [f] his *Master*, and stileth himself his [a] *servant* : Kings are as [h] *Fathers*, and subjects as *sons*; for so King *Ezechias* was a *Father* over the *Fathers* of his people ; even the Priests; and therefore much more over the rest of his subjects. As then Excommunication doth not dissolve the bond of Duty between *Fathers* and *Sons*, of Service between *Masters* and *Servants*, no more doth it the bond of Fidelity between *Princes* and their *Subjects*. And so at length I have proved unto you, that neither supposed Crimes in Princes, as *Tyranny*, *Infidelity*, *Heresie*, *Apostasie*; nor the Episcopal Acts of *Dispensation*, and *Excommunication*; and so, in effect, that nothing can free Subjects from their Fidelity and Allegiance unto their Prince.

Philalethes. *Nothing! The Seal of Confession doth at least in part free some Subjects from special Duties of Obedience unto their Soveraign; as Priests from revealing Treasons, and Conspiracies which they know, as Ghostly Fathers, from the penitent. For if Conspiracies or Treasons be known unto a Priest in Confession, the Bond thereof doth binde him to conceal it , [i] because they are known unto him as unto God, whose Vicar he is in hearing the humble Confessions of repentant Sinners.*

Theodidactus. If Priests in Confessions do understand of Treasons and other enormous Offences , endangering the publick Safety of the Church or Common-weal as GOD, and as his Vicars; then they are to imitate GOD, whom they would represent , in the discovering of these grievous Crimes. For GOD always doth after a miraculous manner , and (as it were) by his own
immediate

Marginal notes:

e *Aquin.in sup.*
qu. 12.
Tolet Inst.
Sacerd.l.1.c.9

f 1 Sam. 24.11
g 1 Sam.
h 2 Chro. 29.
Debora a mother in Israel.
Judg. 5.7.

i *Aquin.in sup.*
qu.11. Art.1.

immediate finger, bring to light crying Sins, when they
are done in ſecret, and for a time are inwrapped in
darkneſs.

Did he not by the Birds of the Air deteſt the Murther of * *Ibycus*? And becauſe the perſons of Princes are
more ſacred than the perſons of private men, GOD
hath made a ſpecial promiſe in his Word, that he will
deteſt * *Curſes*, conceived onely in the heart, againſt
Kings, by the *fowls of the Heaven* (that is) after a ſtrange
and miraculous manner, if by ordinary means they ſhall
not be revealed. And therefore ſome Prieſts of *France*
have deteſted intendments of Treaſon, onely in thought
heard by them in Confeſſion : and the Authors of theſe
intendments have been puniſhed with death. A ' Gentleman of *Normandy* in *France* confeſſed unto a *Frier
Minor*, that he had once a Reſolution to murther King
Francis, and that he repented of his wicked purpoſe.
The Frier gave him Abſolution, but revealed his wicked
purpoſe unto the King : and after deliberation had
thereof in the Parliament of *Paris*, the Gentleman was
executed ; and the Frier not puniſhed with any Cenſure
of the Church for his deteſtion.

Prieſts then are in GODS ſtead, whiles they hear
Penitents confeſſing their ſins, not to conceal theſe ſins
if they be enormous and dangerous unto the publick
State ; but according to their Commiſſion, (*whoſe ſins
ye* ᵐ *remit, they are remitted*) to declare unto them the re-
miſſion of their ſins, as they are offences onely againſt
GOD, and before his heavenly Tribunal.

Philalethes. *But the* Law *of the Church commandeth
Prieſts to conceal all ſuch ſins as come unto their knowledge by
way of Confeſſion.*

Theodidactus. This Law of the Church, is but the Law
of Pope * *Innocent* the Third, cited in the Decretals,
(for he is the moſt ancient Author that the * Romaniſts
can alledge for their *Seal of Confeſſion*:) But were it a

marginalia: * *Ibycus ut periijt, vindex fuit altivolans gens. Auſon.* k Ecclef.10. — l Bodin.lib.2. de Repub.ca.5 — m John 10. — n C. Omnis utriuſq; de Pœniten. & Remiſs. * See Valentia Tom.4. diſt.7. q.13.p.1.

Law of the whole Church, it is but an *Ecclesiastical Law.*
Now if Duties enjoyned by GOD himself in his *Moral,
Law,* as *not to do any manner of work upon the Sabbath day,*
may be omitted by our ° Saviors Commandment, to save,
the life of a beast : May not some things, imposed onely
by an *Ecclesiastical Law,* be neglected for saving the Life
of a King, upon whom so many lives depend ? So that
neither the *Seal of Confession* doth free us from any part
of the duties of Allegiance unto our *Soveraign.*

*Philalethes. If the Bond of Allegiance from Subjects un-
to their Prince is so inviolable, that n thing, no not* the Seal
of Confession, *can dissolve it ; is there no means to stay the
fury of a* Soveraign Commander, *if he should be so tyrannous and profane, as to endeavour to oppress the whole
Church at once, and utterly to extinguish the light of* Christian Religion ?

Theodidactus. Princes in their rage may endeavour
wholly to destroy Christs Church : but in vain ; because Christ hath so built it upon a ᴾ rock, that the
strength and *gates of hell* shall not ever so far prevail
against it, as quite to vanquish it. And when they do
labour to effect so hainous an Impiety, the onely means we
have to appease their fury, is *serious repentance* for our
sins, which have brought this chastisement upon us; and
humble *Prayer* unto GOD, who guideth *the hearts of
Princes like Rivers of waters.* You know how before the
coming of CHRIST, the visible Church was onely
amongst the Jewes ; and that, whiles they were Ca-
ptives under the Persian Monarchs, *Assuerus* at the instigation of *Haman,* sent forth a Decree *to* ᑫ *destroy them
all, both young and old, children and women, in one day.*
Here the whole Church by the barbarous Designment
of *Assuerus,* seemed to be in the very Jaws of Death,
yet they take no Arms, they consult not how to poison
Assuerus or *Haman,* they animate no desperate person
suddenly to stab them ; but there was onely ᵗ *great sorrow
amongst*

● *Mat.* 12.

ᴾ *Mat.* 16.

ᑫ *Esther* 4.

ᵗ *Esth.cap.*4.

amongst them, and fasting, and weeping, many lying in *sack-cloth and ashes,* to humble themselves under the mighty hand of G O D for their sins, and to avert his wrath hanging over their heads, by the cruelty of so bloody a Tyrant.

And the ancient Christians, upon the like occasions, imitated these Jewes. For when they were threatned by *Julian* the Apostata, with an utter Extinction of *Christianity*, they hindred and [*] *repressed him with their tears, having this onely remedy against the Persecuter.* If any therefore are oppressed with the Tyranny of their Supream Governors, *let them* (saith [t] *Sarisburiensis*, even in the darknefs of Popery) *flie unto the patronage of GODS mercy, and with devout Prayer turn away the whip wherewith they are scourged :* [*] *For the sins of offenders, are the strength of Tyrants.*

Philalethes. *To be freed from Tyranny and Oppression in this world, is a temporal benefit : and many times* G O D *hearkneth not unto our prayers for temporal benefits. How then are faithful and loyal Subjects to comfort themselves, against the pressures of mercilesse Tyrants ?*

Theodidactus. Their onely comfort in this case, is that which Saint *Augustine* long since ministred unto them. *The rod of sinners* (saith he, speaking of wicked Masters and Magistrates) *lieth heavy upon the lot of the righteous ; but not for ever. The time will come when one* G O D *shall be acknowledged : The time will come when one* C H R I S T, *appearing in his brightnes, shall gather before him all Nations, and sever them, as a Pastor severeth his Goats from the Sheep, and place his Sheep upon his right hand, and his Goats upon his left. And then thou shalt see many servants,* and subjects, *amongst the sheep, and many masters, and Princes, among the Goats : and again many masters,* and Princes, *amongst the sheep,* and many subjects and servants amongst the ..... that ..... all other helps and comforts do fa..... reched ..... he Day
of

Nazienz. ora. 1. in Julian.

t *Lib. 8. ca. 20*

* *Peccata enim delinquentium sunt vires Tyrannorum.*

of Judgement, the end of all transitory things, will bring an end unto their sorrows.

Philalethes. *With this end of all things, I pray you, let us end this our Conference ; beseeching GOD so to affect the hearts both of* Princes *and* Subjects, *with a serious and frequent cogitation of this last Judgement ; that they in Governing, these in Obeying, both in all their actions, and whatsoever they do, may (with Saint* Hierome*) have the voice of the Archangel always sounding in their eares,* Arise from the dead, and come unto Judgement.

De Reg. & Monacho.

F I N I S.

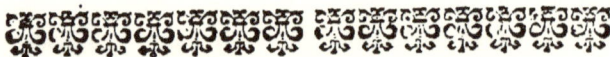

www.ingramcontent.com/pod-product-compliance
Lightning Source LLC
Chambersburg PA
CBHW021431090426
42739CB00009B/1449